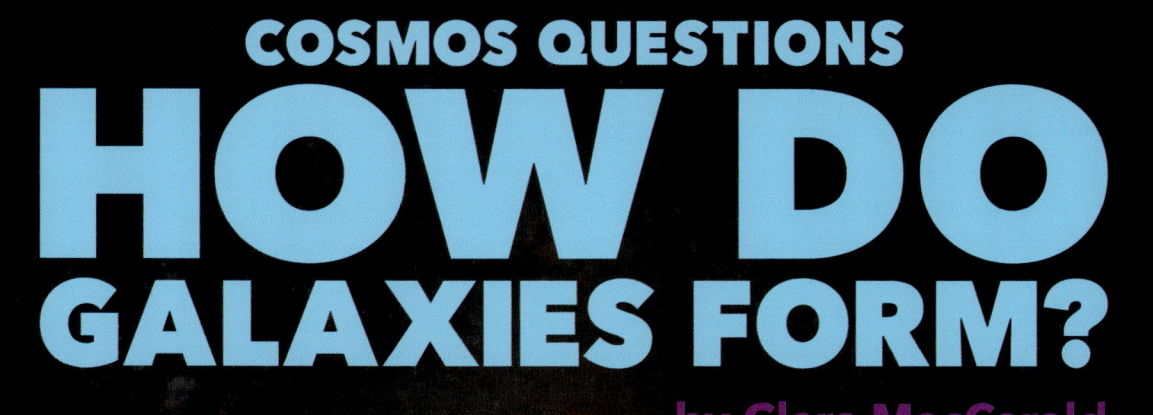

COSMOS QUESTIONS
HOW DO
GALAXIES FORM?

by Clara MacCarald

pogo

Ideas for Parents and Teachers

Pogo Books let children practice reading informational text while introducing them to nonfiction features such as headings, labels, sidebars, maps, and diagrams, as well as a table of contents, glossary, and index.

Carefully leveled text with a strong photo match offers early fluent readers the support they need to succeed.

Before Reading

- "Walk" through the book and point out the various nonfiction features. Ask the student what purpose each feature serves.
- Look at the glossary together. Read and discuss the words.

During Reading

- Have the child read the book independently.
- Invite them to list questions that arise from reading.

After Reading

- Discuss the child's questions. Talk about how they might find answers to those questions.
- Prompt the child to think more. Ask: Why do scientists study galaxies? What could come of learning more about the Milky Way?

Pogo Books are published by Jump!
5357 Penn Avenue South
Minneapolis, MN 55419
www.jumplibrary.com

Jump! is a division of FlutterBee Education Group.

Library of Congress Cataloging-in-Publication Data

Names: MacCarald, Clara, 1979- author.
Title: How do galaxies form? / by Clara MacCarald.
Description: Minneapolis, MN: Jump!, Inc., [2026]
Series: Cosmos questions | Includes index.
Audience: Ages 7-10
Identifiers: LCCN 2024059923 (print)
LCCN 2024059924 (ebook)
ISBN 9798892138499 (hardcover)
ISBN 9798892138505 (paperback)
ISBN 9798892138512 (ebook)
Subjects: LCSH: Galaxies–Juvenile literature.
Galaxies–Formation–Juvenile literature.
Galaxy mergers–Juvenile literature.
Classification: LCC QB857.3 .M23 2026 (print)
LCC QB857.3 (ebook)
DDC 523.1/12–dc23/eng/20250102
LC record available at https://lccn.loc.gov/2024059923
LC ebook record available at https://lccn.loc.gov/2024059924

Editor: Alyssa Sorenson
Designer: Emma Almgren-Bersie

Photo Credits: Goddard/NASA, cover, 16-17; Tryfonov/Adobe Stock, 1; Artsiom P/Shutterstock, 3; Dima Zel/Shutterstock, 4; STScI/NASA, 5; JPL-Caltech/NASA, 6-7; Quality Stock Arts/Adobe Stock, 8; MARK GARLICK/Science Source, 9; MARK PATERNOSTRO/Science Source, 10-11; Declan Hillman/Shutterstock, 12; Shigemi Numazawa/Atlas Photo Bank/Science Source, 13; AstroStar/Shutterstock, 14-15; Paopano/Shutterstock, 18-19 (top), 18-19 (bottom); den-belitsky/iStock, 20-21; FoxPictures/Shutterstock, 23.

Printed in the United States of America at Corporate Graphics in North Mankato, Minnesota.

TABLE OF CONTENTS

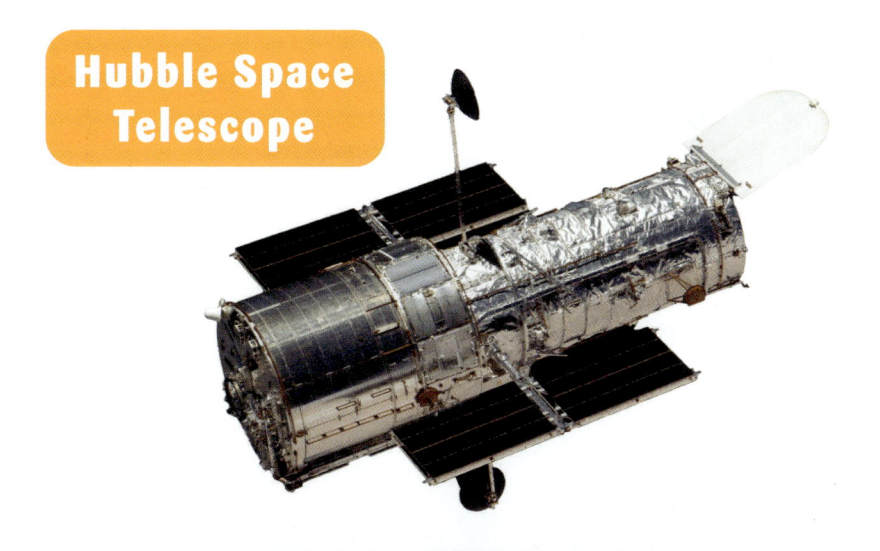

Hubble Space Telescope

CHAPTER 1

WHAT IS A GALAXY?

A galaxy is a large area in space. It has stars and planets. It has gases, **asteroids**, and other space objects, too. A galaxy has its own **gravity**. Gravity keeps everything from floating away.

There are billions of galaxies. Some are very old. Others are still forming.

We live in the Milky Way. This galaxy is large. It is 100,000 **light-years** across!

DID YOU KNOW?

The Milky Way has hundreds of billions of stars. The Sun is one. It is the center of our **solar system**.

Milky Way

Earth

CHAPTER 2

THE BIRTH OF GALAXIES

Around 13.8 billion years ago, the **universe** did not exist. Instead, there was a small fireball. It grew quickly! The universe was born. This event is called the big bang.

protogalaxy

Matter spread out. Some formed clumps. When clumps got too big, their gravity made them fall in on themselves. This made them very hot. Stars formed! These young star systems are called protogalaxies. Protogalaxies ran into each other. They turned into galaxies. The crashes led to more forming stars.

Sometimes stars form slowly. This makes a **spiral**-shaped galaxy. Other times, stars form quickly. That makes an elliptical galaxy. There are irregular galaxies, too. They can form when two galaxies crash into each other. Elliptical galaxies can form this way, too.

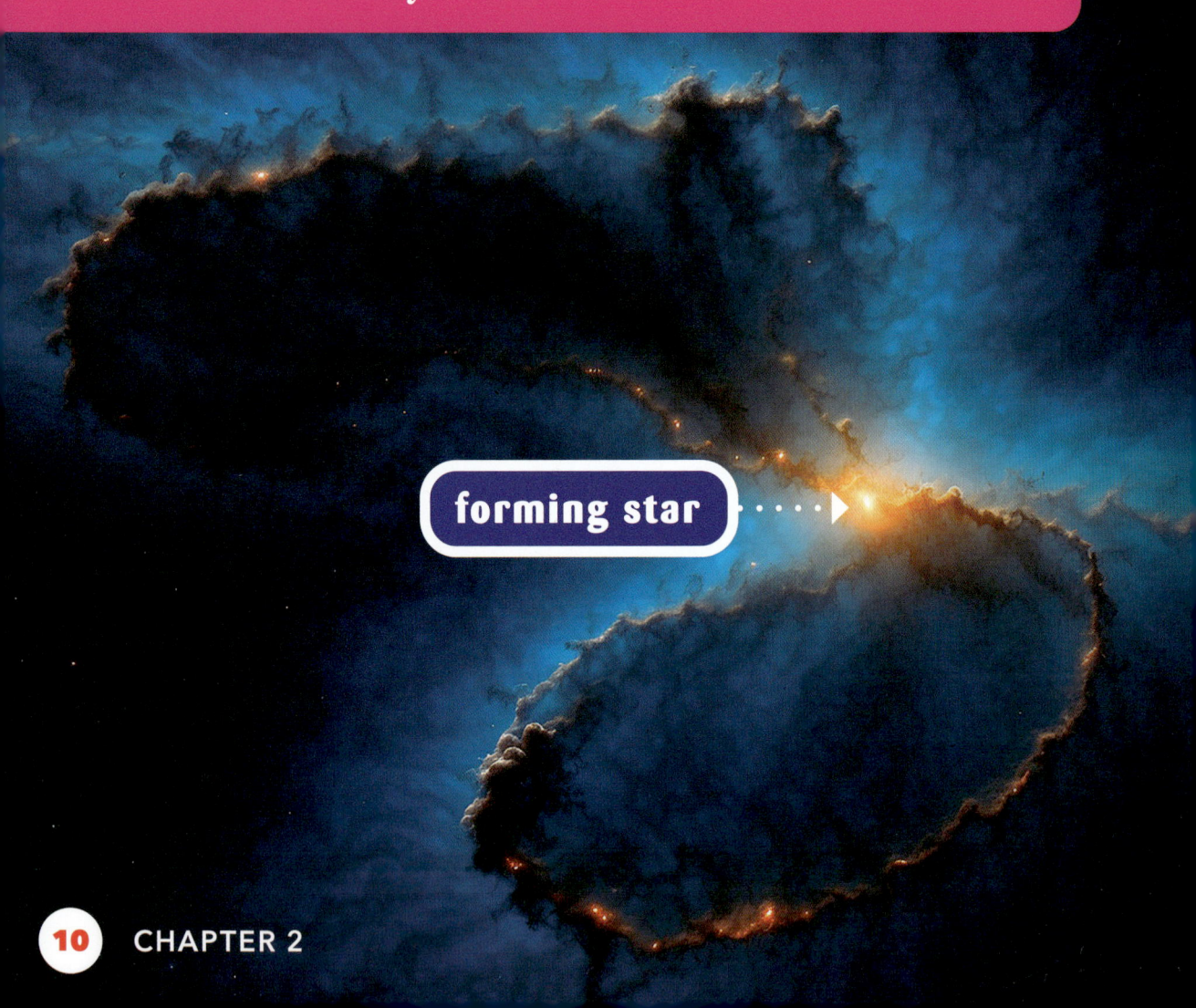

forming star

The Milky Way is a spiral galaxy. What do the types look like? Take a look!

SPIRAL GALAXY

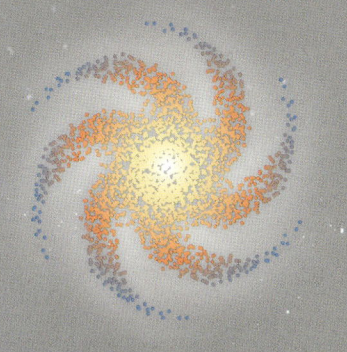

- curved arms
- looks like a pinwheel

ELLIPTICAL GALAXY

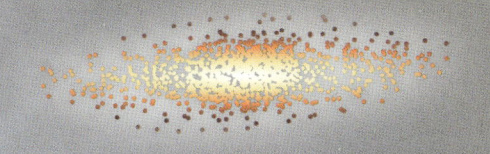

- round or oval shaped

IRREGULAR GALAXY

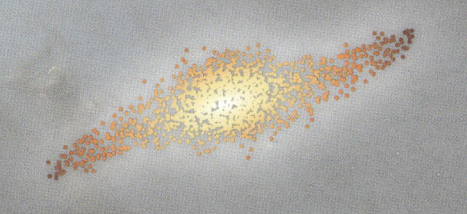

- does not have a clear shape

CHAPTER 3

CRASHING GALAXIES

Galaxies move in space. They get close to other galaxies. Galaxies have gravity. They pull on each other. This makes them get even closer!

Eventually, they **collide**. Stars and planets in the two galaxies do not hit each other. Why? There is a lot of empty space! Still, gravity whips space objects around. It might even rip them apart.

Andromeda galaxy

The Andromeda galaxy is close to the Milky Way. It is headed toward us! The two galaxies will collide. When? Not for another 4 billion years. The crash will make an elliptical galaxy.

DID YOU KNOW?

What will happen when the Milky Way and Andromeda collide? The Sun will be pushed to a different area in the new galaxy. But Earth will not be destroyed.

Galaxy crashes bring gases together.
The gases form huge clouds.
Stars are born from them!

Scientists study galaxies. How? They use powerful telescopes. The Hubble Space Telescope **orbits** Earth. It looks out at the universe. It gathers **data**.

DID YOU KNOW?

The James Webb Space Telescope is the biggest space telescope. It studies how early galaxies formed.

Hubble Space Telescope

James Webb Space Telescope

Some data includes light. Light takes time to travel. Andromeda is 2.5 million light-years away. That means the light we see from it is 2.5 million years old! By studying this light, scientists learn about our universe.

Galaxies give us clues about how our universe formed. They show us how it is changing, too!

ACTIVITIES & TOOLS

TRY THIS!

MAKE A GALAXY

Make a spiral galaxy with this fun activity!

What You Need:

- 1 sheet of black construction paper
- ruler
- scissors
- pencil
- white marker or gel pen
- glue stick
- pin

1. **Draw a square on your paper. Each side should be six inches (15 centimeters) long. Cut out the square.**

2. **Using a white marker or gel pen, decorate both sides of the paper with stars.**

3. **Draw a line from each corner to the center. This will make four triangles.**

4. **Cut about 2.5 inches (6 cm) of each line starting at the corner.**

5. **Fold the right side of each triangle into the center. Do not press hard.**

6. **Use glue to hold down the tips. Let the glue dry.**

7. **Push a pin through the center.**

8. **Press the pin's tip into the pencil's eraser.**

9. **Blow on one of the galaxy's arms. The galaxy will start spinning!**

GLOSSARY

asteroids: Small, rocky objects that move through space.

collide: To crash together forcefully.

data: Information collected so something can be done with it.

gravity: The force that pulls things toward the center of a space object and keeps them from floating away.

light-years: Measures of distance in space. One light-year is 5.9 trillion miles (9.5 trillion kilometers).

matter: Something that has weight and takes up space, such as a solid, liquid, or gas.

orbits: Travels in a circular path around something.

solar system: The Sun, together with its orbiting bodies, as well as asteroids, comets, and meteors.

spiral: Winding in a curve around a fixed point.

universe: All existing matter and space.

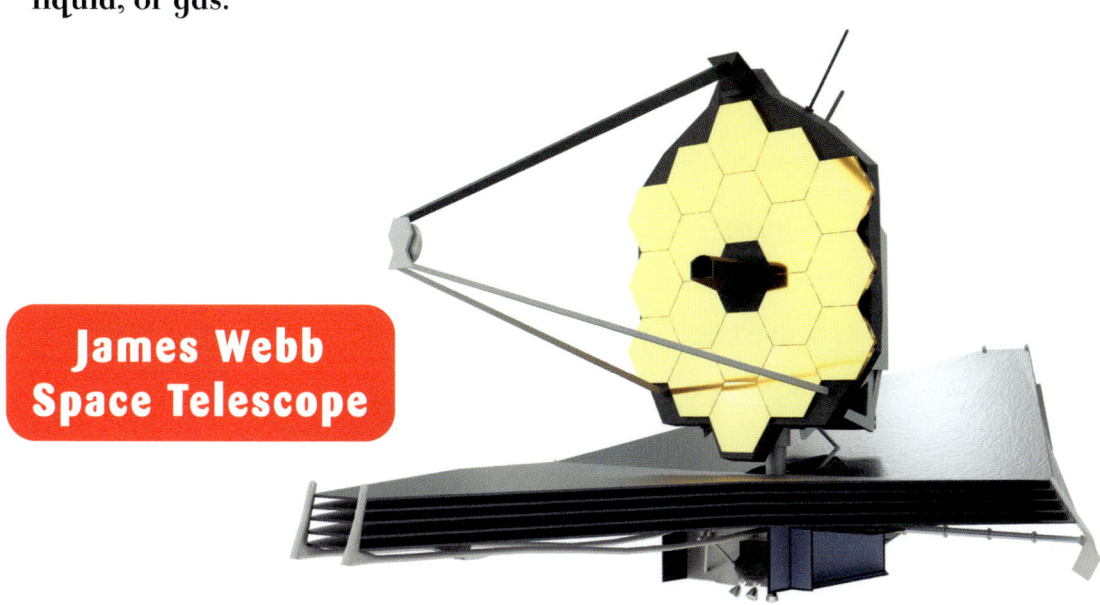

James Webb Space Telescope

INDEX

TO LEARN MORE

Finding more information is as easy as 1, 2, 3.

1. **Go to www.factsurfer.com**
2. **Enter "galaxies" into the search box.**
3. **Choose your book to see a list of websites.**

FACT SURFER